The Missions of California

Mission
San Francisco de Asís

Kathleen J. Edgar and Susan E. Edgar

The Rosen Publishing Group's
PowerKids Press™
New York

Published in 2000 by The Rosen Publishing Group, Inc.
29 East 21st Street, New York, NY 10010

Copyright © 2000 by The Rosen Publishing Group, Inc.

Photo Credits and Photo Illustrations: pp. 1, 19, 23, 28, 31, 46, 47, 48, 49, 50 by Cristina Taccone; pp. 5, 17, 18 Santa Barbara Mission Archive - Library; p. 7 The Bridgeman Art Library; pp. 8, 16 CORBIS; pp. 9, 11, 13, 26, 35 by Michael Ward; pp. 12, 44 © The Granger Collection; p. 15 Courtesy of National Park Service, Cabrillo National Monument; p. 20 Seaver Center for Western History Research, Los Angeles County Museum of Natural History; pp. 24, 34, 49 Courtesy of Mission San Francisco de Asís; pp. 30, 36, 38, 40 by Tim Hall; p. 32 © Superstock; pp. 37, 42, 45 CORBIS/Bettmann; pp. 52, 57 by Christine Innamorato.

First Edition

Book Design: Danielle Primiceri

Layout: Michael de Guzman

Editorial Consultant Coordinator: Karen Fontanetta, M.A., Curator, Mission San Miguel Arcángel
Historical Photo Consultants: Thomas L. Davis, M.Div., M.A.
                         Michael K. Ward, M.A.

Edgar, Kathleen J.
      Mission San Francisco de Asís / by Kathleen J. Edgar and Susan E. Edgar.
         p.   cm. — (The missions of California)
      Includes index.
      Summary: Discusses the Mission of San Francisco de Asís from its founding in 1776 to the present day, including the reasons for Spanish colonization in California and the effects of the Ohlone Indians.
      ISBN 0-8239-5492-7 (lib.bdg.)
      1. San Francisco de Asís Mission (San Francisco, Calif.)—History—Juvenile literature. 2. Spanish mission buildings—California—San Francisco—History Juvenile literature. 3. Franciscans—California—San Francisco—History Juvenile literature. 4. Ohlone Indians—Missions—California—San Francisco Bay Area—History Juvenile literature. 5 California—History—To 1846 Juvenile literature. [1. San Francsico de Asís Mission (San Francisco, Calif.)—History. 2. Missions—California. 3. Ohlone Indians—Missions. Indians of North America—Missions—California. 5. California—History—To 1846.]   I. Edgar, Susan E. II. Title. III. Series.
F869.S393E24   1999
979.4'61—dc21   99-25062
                                                                 CIP

Manufactured in the United States of America

Contents

The Spanish Arrive in Alta California

On a busy street in the heart of San Francisco stands a church called Mission Dolores Basilica. Two ornately carved spires, each topped with a cross, rise above the entranceway. Yet, next to this modern-looking structure sits a smaller, older building, with simple white walls and a rust-colored tile roof. This building is the original church of Mission Dolores, part of Mission San Francisco de Asís. Mission San Francisco de Asís, usually called Mission Dolores, was the sixth of 21 missions, or religious settlements, founded by the Spanish between 1769 and 1823 in California.

Steps leading up from the sidewalk stop at thick wooden doors. Above the entrance is a balcony supported by four massive columns. Suspended in the wall behind the balcony are three bronze bells made in Mexico in the 1790s and brought north to California by Spanish missionaries.

The Spanish first became interested in California after Christopher Columbus discovered the lands that Europeans called the New World (North America, South America, and Central America) in 1492. At that time, Spain was a world power that was eager to explore the New World in search of gold and other riches. The Spanish king wanted to claim these lands and their resources for the Spanish empire. He also wanted to spread the Catholic religion throughout the world. Catholicism is a Christian religion based on the teachings of Jesus Christ and the Bible. In addition to wanting to help the Roman Catholic Church with gold and other resources from the New World, the Spanish wanted to teach the many Indians living in the New World about Christianity.

In 1542, Juan Rodríguez Cabrillo became one of the first Spanish explorers to reach the western coast of North America. At that time, the

The original church of Mission Dolores. ▶

4

name "Californias" described both the area that is now the region of Mexico called the Baja Peninsula and the area that is the state of California. The Baja Peninsula was known as Baja (meaning "lower") California, while what is now the state of California was called Alta (meaning "upper") California.

When Cabrillo sailed to Alta California, he saw many California Indians living along the coast. The Spanish crew traded cloth and trinkets with them for acorn bread and berries. Cabrillo described the people of Alta California in his journals, calling them friendly, generous, and peaceful. Members of his expedition planted a cross in the ground near San Diego, claiming the land for Spain.

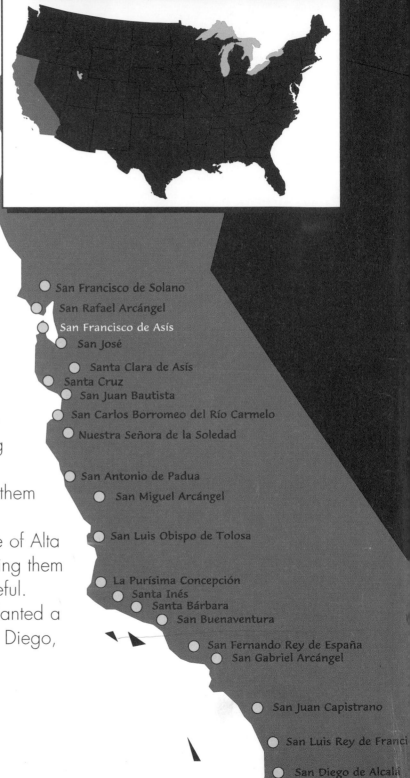

San Francisco de Solano
San Rafael Arcángel
San Francisco de Asís
San José
Santa Clara de Asís
Santa Cruz
San Juan Bautista
San Carlos Borromeo del Río Carmelo
Nuestra Señora de la Soledad
San Antonio de Padua
San Miguel Arcángel
San Luis Obispo de Tolosa
La Purísima Concepción
Santa Inés
Santa Bárbara
San Buenaventura
San Fernando Rey de España
San Gabriel Arcángel
San Juan Capistrano
San Luis Rey de Franci
San Diego de Alcalá

Thirty-seven years later, Sir Francis Drake, the British explorer, sailed into a harbor just north of San Francisco. He claimed the land for Great Britain, calling it Nova Albion (New England). The British sent settlers to establish a colony in Nova Albion but a fleet of Spanish ships turned them away off the coast of South America, which was then controlled by the Spanish. It was almost 200 years later that Spain sent its first settlers to Alta California.

Mission San Francisco de Asís was named after the founder of the Franciscan religious order, Saint Francis of Assisi. Born in 1182 in the town of Assisi, Italy, Francis lived a wealthy lifestyle until one day when he decided to cast aside his riches to live in poverty and holiness. Others were impressed with his religious devotion and began to follow his example. Together they formed the Franciscan order, a segment of the Roman Catholic Church, and observed a strict lifestyle that included chastity, poverty, and obedience. Unlike others in his day, Francis believed that all creatures were important. Paintings and statues usually show him holding birds or with animals near him.

The Ohlone Indians

California Indians populated the land of Alta California in hundreds of small villages. They lived in tribes of 80 to 100 people.

The Indians living near the San Francisco Bay area were known as the Ohlone. Each tribe of Ohlone had its own territory and village where the tribe lived most of the time. Occasionally different tribes would fight over the land. Sometimes the tribe would move to a temporary site, usually to collect acorns for food. They built their houses out of willow branches or reeds that they tied together.

The Ohlone were hunters and gatherers. The men did the hunting and fishing. They used bows and arrows to hunt game. They made bows from strong, flexible tree branches and bowstrings from vegetables stalks or animal sinew. Arrowheads and spearheads were

The Ohlone sometimes disguised themselves to fool the deer they were hunting.

◀ *The Ohlone Indians.*

carved out of obsidian, which is a very hard kind of glass. Though obsidian wasn't native to the area where the Ohlone lived, they traded nuts and clam shells to get the precious material from other tribes.

The Ohlone men used baskets and nets woven from cattails, reeds, and willow branches to catch fish and grasshoppers. The women made these baskets and gathered food, such as clams, oysters, onions, carrots, strawberries, mushrooms, and grapes for the tribe to eat. They also used baskets for food storage, hauling water, and cooking.

Everyone helped to harvest acorns in the fall. Acorns were important to the Ohlone's diet. Once the acorns were gathered, the women ground the acorns into flour using bowl-shaped rocks and grinding stones. Acorns are poisonous, so the women had to wash the flour by pouring water over it about 10 times. Then they were able to use the flour to make bread, mush, and cake.

The Ohlone also used items found in the area to make their clothing. In the warmer months, the men wore little or no clothing at all. The women wore skirts designed like aprons that tied together in the back. When the weather cooled, both men and women draped animal hides over their shoulders like a cape or robe. Sometimes they applied mud to their bodies to help keep them warm.

Both men and women wore their hair long, usually braided or in ponytails. Some tied their hair into knots on top of their heads. They wore jewelry made from shells, leather, wood, bone, and feathers. Many Ohlone painted their faces for further decoration.

The Indians ground acorns into flour in stone bowls.

The Ohlone Indians decorated themselves with paints and accessories.

According to their religion, the Ohlone respected people, the land, and all creatures of the Earth. They believed that many spirits were at work in nature. One group, called the Miwok, believed that the coyote and frog created the Earth by scattering sand into the ocean to create the land for the people to live on. The Ohlone believed other spirits brought sickness. They relied on shamans (medicine men) to heal the sick using herbs and other remedies.

Singing, dancing, and playing games were favorite pastimes of the Ohlone. They made their own musical instruments. They made rattles out of dried gourds and seeds and carved whistles out of wood and bone.

The Ohlone way of life was altered forever when the Spanish arrived to build Mission San Francisco de Asís in the 1700s.

Shamans sometimes wore feathers and face paint, as shown in this picture. ▶

The Mission System

The Spanish mission system was already in place in other parts of the New World when the Spanish came to California. More than 200 years before the founding of Mission San Francisco de Asís, missionaries, soldiers, and settlers were sent to parts of North America, Central America, and South America. The Spanish established a capital, which they called Mexico City, and called the surrounding lands where they had established themselves New Spain. Today this land belongs to the country of Mexico.

The Spanish thought that the California Indians were savages because the Indians lived much differently from the Europeans. The Indians wore few clothes, were not educated in schools, and did not believe in the Christian god. The Spanish thought American Indians should adopt the Spanish lifestyle and religion and that these changes were in the best interests of the Indians. The government in New Spain developed procedures for colonizing the area and teaching the Indians about Christianity.

Though the Spanish missionaries may have had good intentions, their belief that the American Indians were inferior was unfounded. They presumed that because the American Indians had a different culture from their own, they had no culture. Of course, this kind of thinking is unacceptable today, and the Spanish treatment of the American Indians is now considered unfair and misguided.

Spain sent several explorers, including Juan Rodríguez Cabrillo, to the New World. ▶

▲

The Spanish taught the Ohlone how to raise livestock.

Starting the Missions

The religious people involved in the missions were members of a Catholic order called the Franciscans. Friars of this order (called *frays* in Spanish) devoted their lives to helping the poor and sick and spreading their faith. Missionaries, soldiers, and settlers worked together to establish communities, called missions. At the missions, friars taught the California Indians how to raise livestock, how to plant and harvest crops, and how to work in such trades as weaving, carpentry, blacksmithing, soapmaking, candlemaking, and leatherworking. They also taught them about the Christian religion.

While the missionaries taught the Indians, the soldiers took possession of the land, guarding it by building presidios (or military fortresses). The few other settlers who came to California cleared the land for planting and began building towns and ranches.

The Spanish government estimated that it would take roughly 10 years to train the Indians in Spanish work methods and religion. The mission lands would then be released to the Indians for them to operate on their own. The land would belong to Spain, and the Indians would become tax-paying Spanish citizens. The Spanish called this process secularization. Once secularization took place, the friars would move to a new location and start a new mission.

By the 1700s, many missions were thriving in Baja California. The Spanish set their sights on Alta California because they feared they would lose the land to Russian and British settlers.

This is what many presidios looked like.

The Founders of Mission San Francisco de Asís

Several men were instrumental in the founding of the Alta California mission chain, including Mission San Francisco de Asís. Among them were missionaries and military men of New Spain.

▲ *The church at Mission San Francisco de Asís.*

Fray Serra

Fray Junípero Serra was the first president of the Alta California missions. He was born in Majorca, Spain, on November 24, 1713. He became a priest in 1737 and spent some years teaching philosophy. He knew that he wanted to spread his faith, so he later moved to New Spain and was put in charge of five missions in Baja California. When he was 55 years old, Serra was chosen by the Roman Catholic Church to head the Alta California missions. His first task was to found two missions in southern Alta California. He established one in San Diego and another in Monterey, more than 450 miles to the north. Though he was not actually present for the founding ceremony at Mission San Francisco de Asís, as mission president Serra was credited with its founding. He died on August 28, 1784, at Mission San Carlos Borromeo del Río Carmelo (near Monterey), where he had made his headquarters.

A statue of Fray Serra. ▶

Captain Portolá

Captain Don Gaspár de Portolá was the first military leader of Alta California. Born in 1723, in Balaguer, Spain, he joined the military at a young age and eventually became a captain in the Spanish army. He was appointed governor of the Californias by the Spanish

Don Gaspár de Portolá. ▶

government in 1767. Portolá was in charge of the five expeditions that traveled to Alta California in 1769 to claim the land for Spain and to help Serra build the missions. He then set off for Monterey and explored the area that would become San Francisco. In 1770, he retired to New Spain.

Captain Rivera

Captain Fernando de Rivera y Moncada played an important role in the founding of Mission San Francisco de Asís. He began his military career in 1742. After helping to establish missions in Baja California, Rivera led one of Portolá's expeditions to San Diego and then on to Monterey. In 1773, Rivera was appointed governor of Alta California, and in 1774 he traveled to the San Francisco Bay area with Fray Francisco Palóu to select a site for the mission and presidio to be built there.

After retiring as governor in 1776, he led several expeditions of soldiers and settlers to Alta California. He was killed in 1781, during an Indian revolt at San Pedro y San Pablo, one of the branch missions of San Francisco de Asís.

Fray Palóu

Fray Francisco Palóu was the first friar to take charge of Mission San Francisco de Asís. Born on January 22, 1723, in Majorca, Spain, he became a friar in 1746. Like his former teacher, Fray Serra, Palóu became a missionary in New Spain. He arrived in Alta California in 1773 at Mission San Diego de Alcalá. In 1774, he traveled with Captain Rivera to select a site for the sixth mission. In June 1776 Palóu established Mission San Francisco de Asís, where he remained in charge until 1785. After Serra's death in 1784 Palóu served briefly as mission president, but returned to Mexico City in 1785 as the head of the College of San Fernando. He wrote several books, including *The Founding of the First California Missions* and *The Life of Fray Junípero Serra.*

Captain Anza

Born in New Spain in July 1736, Captain Juan Bautista de Anza was the son of an explorer and continued his father's work by establishing supply routes. Anza joined the military when he was 15. By the time he was 23, he was put in charge of the presidio in a place called Tubac, in the Sonora region of New Spain. He died on December 19, 1788.

Several of the founding fathers of the mission are buried in the graveyard at Mission San Francisco de Asís. ▶

The Journey to San Francisco

After the first mission, Mission San Diego de Alcalá, was founded, four more missions were established during the next few years. These were Mission San Carlos Borromeo del Río Carmelo, Mission San Gabriel Arcángel, Mission San Antonio de Padua, and Mission San Luis Obispo. When the Spanish came to found these missions, they brought many things they would need, including cattle, sheep, seeds for planting, wine, tools, and religious articles. Often, the supplies they brought were not enough. The men were frequently faced with food shortages. Captain Rivera was sent to New Spain several times over the next few years to bring supplies back to Alta California.

In November 1774, Rivera, who had recently been appointed governor of Alta California, left Monterey with Fray Palóu and several soldiers to select a site for the sixth mission and presidio. They found an ideal spot in what is now called the San Francisco Bay area. However, Rivera was afraid there wouldn't be enough soldiers to protect the land and the mission once it had been established, so he stalled the founding of the mission for two years.

Meanwhile, Captain Anza was establishing the supply route from Tabac, New Spain, to Monterey, a trail that was about 1,200 miles long. In 1775, Anza led a caravan of 40 soldiers, 140 settlers (including women and children), 1,000 cattle, and 120 pack mules along his route, carrying supplies for Mission San Francisco de Asís. During the journey north, several people died of diseases, and nine babies were born. The travelers arrived at the presidio in Monterey on March 10, 1776.

◀ *Many California Indians lived in the area where Mission San Francisco de Asís would be founded.*

After the travelers had rested for a few months, Lieutenant José Joachin Moraga and Fray Palóu led about 180 settlers from Anza's group to the San Francisco area. They brought 200 cattle and several Indians from Mission San Carlos Borromeo del Río Carmelo as *vaqueros* (cowboys or ranch hands).

In his writings, Fray Palóu described the group's arrival in the location where they would found Mission San Francisco de Asís: "On June 27 the expedition arrived near its destination. The commander, therefore, ordered the camp to be pitched on the bank of a lagoon...named Nuestra Señora de los Dolores.... No sooner had the expedition gone into camp than many pagan [non-Christian] Indians appeared in a friendly manner and with expressions of joy at our coming. Their satisfaction increased when they experienced the kindness with which we treated them and when they received the little trinkets we would give them in order to attract them, such as beads.... They would repeat their visits and bring little things...such as shellfish and wild seeds."

The Indians' way of life was greatly changed by the arrival of the Spanish. ▶

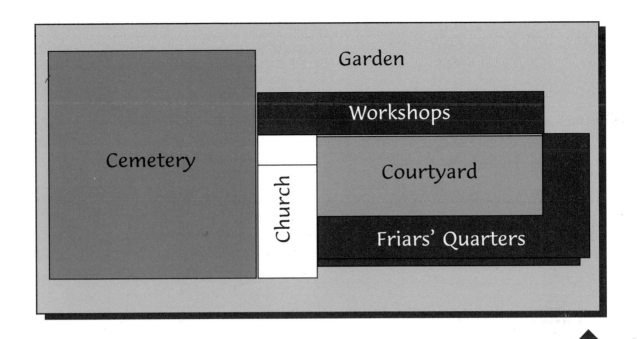

This is a map of the layout of the mission.

Building Begins

On June 29, 1776, Captain Moraga and his men started to build a temporary chapel. Fray Palóu conducted Catholic ritual called a Mass and blessed the site of Mission San Francisco de Asís. Soon after, the soldiers and settlers from New Spain began building the presidio overlooking the bay. Once the construction was well underway, several of the workers began construction of more permanent structures on the site of the mission.

As the friars and soldiers built, some of the Ohlone ventured to the site. They were drawn in by the Spanish trinkets and tools, most of which were unlike anything they had ever seen before.

Founding Ceremonies

The official dedication of the mission was held on October 9, 1776, just days after the religious holiday honoring Saint Francis of Assisi, for whom the mission was named. During the ceremony, the participants erected a cross at the mission site. Then they sang, rang bells, and fired off muskets and cannons.

Bells like these were used in the founding ceremony.

The blasts of the cannon and muskets fired during the founding ceremonies scared off the Ohlone, who were unfamiliar with such weapons. The Ohlone eventually returned to see what the Spanish were doing. Again, they were attracted by the gifts the missionaries and settlers offered them. The Spanish had tools, fabrics, glass beads, and other goods that fascinated the Ohlone.

The Indians watched as the Spanish used tools made of metal to cut down trees to make building supports. Some of the Ohlone wanted to try these tools and offered to help. The Spanish needed the Ohlones' help to build and were determined to keep them working. They knew that working together to build the mission buildings was a good opportunity to start teaching the Ohlone about Spanish work methods.

To build the structures, the Spanish and the Ohlone gathered the materials they needed. The area was rich in forests of redwood and other trees. They chopped down many trees and cut them into planks for the buildings. The workers used *carretas* (small wooden carts pulled by oxen or mules) to move the lumber to the mission site.

The workers made bricks for the walls out of adobe, a mixture of clay, water, straw, and sometimes manure. The missionaries showed the Ohlone men, women, and children how to mix the ingredients together by stomping it with their feet or by having animals stomp it down. They poured the mixture into wooden molds to make rectangular bricks. They let the bricks dry in the sun until they were hard. Then they built walls, using mud to hold the bricks in place. They laid the bricks side by side, one row on top of another.

Indians working on the mission.

The Ohlone showed the missionaries and settlers how to make buildings using reeds and twigs bundled together and plastered with clay to keep the rain out. The Spanish called this kind of construction *palizada*.

The mission in San Francisco took many years to build. During the first few years, the workers constructed many buildings out of adobe, including living quarters and offices for the missionaries, dormitories for the neophytes living at the mission, and a church. They also built a granary and several kitchens made of *palizada*. Several of these kitchens were called "*pozole* kitchens" and were used solely for making *pozole* (a stew made of vegetables, grain, and sometimes meat).

As the building continued, the workers constructed stables, carpentry shops, work rooms, and a new church. They also planted crops and fruit tree orchards in fields near the mission complex. A farming station, called a *labor*, was established in the San Pedro Valley in 1786. It was used as a branch of the mission and called San Pedro y San Pablo. This *labor* included a chapel, living quarters, storage rooms, and granaries. In 1790, approximately 300 Christian Indians lived there.

By 1788, the neophytes had started to dig an irrigation ditch to bring water from nearby Lake Dolores to the crop fields at San Pedro y San Pablo. The first house for an Indian family was built in 1790. Over the next 10 years, nearly 100 Indian houses were constructed. In the 1790s, the workers added a gristmill, a pottery kiln, and a bathhouse.

Although the mission was named for Saint Francis of Assisi, it is often called Mission Dolores, after a river and lake by the same name in the area. The river, lake, and mission carry the name of Dolores because the Spanish arrived in the area on the day when Catholics honor the Virgin Mary. *Dolores* is the Spanish word for "sorrow." In Spanish, the Virgin Mary is sometimes called Nuestra Señora de los Dolores, meaning Our Lady of Sorrows.

31

Daily Life at the Mission

The Ohlone who converted to Catholicism and moved into Mission San Francisco de Asís followed a strict daily schedule established and enforced by the missionaries. As the sun began to rise, the mission residents awoke to the sound of bells ringing in the *campanario* (bell tower). Then they were brought together to go to church for Mass, morning prayers, and church lessons.

These religious duties were followed by breakfast. For a time, the neophytes at Mission San Francisco de Asís were only given dry grain to eat, while neophytes at most missions were fed *atole*, a porridge made of corn or grain.

After breakfast, it was time for work. Jobs were given to both men and women. In addition to cooking, the Ohlone women made baskets, soap, and cloth. The Spanish brought European looms so they could teach the women how to weave fabric. The women used the fabric to make clothes for the men, children, soldiers, and themselves. They also made wool blankets to keep people warm at night.

The Spanish taught the Ohlone men how to farm, raise livestock, and create goods for trade. Among the skills they learned were tanning, leatherworking, carpentry, blacksmithing, and construction. The missionaries often brought in craftsmen from missions in New Spain to teach these trades. During the day, some of the friars worked side by side with the neophytes.

◀ *The Indians worked hard at the mission.*

At Mission San Francisco de Asís, the Ohlone raised livestock, including cattle, sheep, mules, and horses. They planted wheat, corn, beans, barley, peas, lentils, and fruit trees. Eventually, the Ohlone women began to use corn and wheat flour rather than acorn flour. When time permitted, they still gathered nuts and edible plants, especially in the early years of the mission.

The workers took a break for lunch. Eventually, meals of dry grain were replaced by *pozole*. After lunch they took a rest or nap called a *siesta*. Then work resumed for a short period in the afternoon.

Another Mass was held before supper. The evening concluded with more prayers, church instruction, Spanish-language lessons, and some time to relax. The Indians enjoyed singing, dancing, and playing games during their free time.

Fiestas, or festivals, were sometimes held. These broke up the routine of mission life. The Catholics held *fiestas* in honor of various saints, weddings, births, and important events in church history. The Ohlone were able to observe some of their traditional ceremonies, too. The friars believed that such rituals were against

Sometimes the Spanish had bullfights during their fiestas.

Catholic teachings, but the friars allowed the Indian rituals to occur because they wanted to keep things peaceful at the mission. On one occasion, the friars even used a traditional Ohlone dance to impress a Russian expedition headed by Otto Von Kotzebue that came to the mission in 1816. The missionaries asked the Ohlone to perform their native dances in their traditional clothing for the visitors.

A Hard Life

Life presented challenges for everyone at the mission. The Ohlone were often frustrated and angry at being kept on the mission grounds, sometimes against their will. Many felt that they had been unfairly brought into mission life and did not want to become Catholic, follow the friars' rules, or be subject to the abusive treatment of the Spanish soldiers.

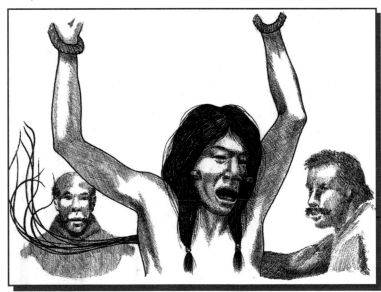

The Spanish friars and soldiers often felt isolated being so far away from their friends, family, and homeland. The Spanish had to adjust to a different climate, environment, and way of life. They didn't have many of

▲
Indians were often punished for disobedience by the Spanish soldiers.

The Indians were taught Spanish farming methods.

the comforts they had known in Spain and New Spain. Living quarters were rustic and included only a simple wooden cot with a single, coarse blanket. The food was often bland.

The life of a missionary was filled with many tasks. In addition to their religious lessons, missionaries taught the Ohlone about Spanish trades and farming and ranching techniques. They were responsible for performing religious services, such as Mass, funerals, weddings, and baptisms. The missionaries also had to manage the soldiers, who were often rough.

The government in New Spain also required the friars to keep records of life at the mission. These records help today's historians understand a lot about how the Indians lived and worked at Mission San Francisco de Asís. For example, these records show that in 1820 at Mission San Francisco de Asís, 1,242 neophytes lived at the mission. In 1832, the mission owned 3,500 sheep, 5,000 cattle, 1,000 horses, and 18 mules. The friars also noted a total of 2,043 marriages, 5,166 deaths, and 6,898 baptisms in a 60-year period. From 1785 to 1832, the workers harvested more than 70,000 bushels of barley, 18,000 bushels of corn, and 120,000 bushels of wheat.

The friars baptized Indian children into the Catholic faith.

The Decline of Mission San Francisco de Asís

Conflict

The Ohlones' frustration and growing resentment of the mission system caused tensions to flare up frequently at the mission. Besides the fact that all neophytes were forbidden to leave the mission and would be severely punished if they tried, daily life was strict and labor-intensive, and many Ohlone were restless and unhappy.

Also, single Indian girls and women were required to live separately from the other residents. They lived in dormitories, called *monjerios*, which were locked at night to keep the girls in and others out. The mission doors were also locked at night. Many of the Ohlone tried to escape. The Ohlone often hid out in the Contra Costa, the opposite side of the bay. Those who escaped and were caught were rounded up and returned to the mission, where they were punished. Typical punishments included whippings and beatings.

Yet many Ohlone managed to get away from Mission San Francisco de Asís. Some wanted to join tribes outside of the mission that were living a traditional lifestyle or go to other settlements in the area and try to live free lives there. In 1795 approximately 280 Indians ran away, followed by more than 200 over the next year. The soldiers grew tired of hunting down runaways, which frustrated the missionaries, because they wanted the Ohlone brought back to the mission. Sometimes neophytes were sent to search for runaways. In one search in the 1790s, about seven neophytes were killed by other neophytes of Mission San Francisco de Asís outside of the mission complex.

◀ *Many of the missionaries treated the Indians like children.*

39

Disease

The San Francisco climate was often cool and damp. As a result, much of the soil in the area was poor for growing crops. The neophytes and missionaries had difficulty growing crops and often didn't have enough food.

The climate also contributed to sickness and disease at Mission San Francisco de Asís. Many of the Indians found themselves becoming sick with diseases common in Spain but unknown in Alta California. Their bodies had not built up any resistance to diseases such as measles and smallpox. In March 1806, the mission was hit with a measles outbreak that resulted in 471 deaths.

European diseases brought sickness and death to the California Indians.

Those who survived the epidemic had trouble recovering in the San Francisco climate. They also had trouble because of the living conditions at the mission. Many of the living quarters were cramped, especially the *monjerios*. The adobe buildings were damp inside and caused the residents to develop breathing problems. The mission's poor sanitation systems attracted bugs and rodents. In 1816, Otto Von Kotzebue, the Russian explorer who had visited the mission, wrote, "The uncleanliness in these barracks baffles description, and this is perhaps the cause of the great mortality." While on an expedition to the area in the 1820s, the explorer Frederick William Beechey wrote about the neophyte homes. "Their hovels afforded scarcely any protection against the weather, and were black with smoke: Some of the Indians were sleeping on the greasy floor."

Disease hit the neophyte population at Mission San Francisco de Asís very hard and caused many deaths. Some of the neophytes began to doubt their new Christian faith, if they had not done so already. In 1817 the friars sent the sick to an *asistencia* (branch mission) called San Rafael that they had built on the north side of the bay. At San Rafael the sick were able to recover in the warm sunshine. Fray Luís Gil, who had studied medicine, was placed in charge of the *asistencia*. More than 300 people were sent there during the first year.

Secularization and Statehood

In 1810, residents of New Spain began a war to gain their independence from the Spanish government. This war went on for 11 years. During this time, the people living at the missions were required to work harder to supply food and clothing to the Spanish soldiers. In 1821, the people of New Spain gained their independence from Spain and formed a new nation called Mexico. As a result of this upheaval, the missions in Alta California fell under the authority of this new government.

The Mexican government was not happy with the state of the missions. Some officials thought that the Indians living at the missions were being treated like slaves. Others saw the richness of the mission lands and wanted to take them so they could become wealthy. In August 1833, the Mexican government finally decided to secularize the missions. However, secularization did not occur as the Spanish had planned it. Rather than turning the mission land and property over to the converted Indians, the Mexican government's Secularization Laws of 1833 gave control of the mission property to the Mexican government.

A small portion of the mission lands, buildings, livestock, and crops were distributed to the Indians. Much of the area was taken over by local landowners who either took the land outright, bought land from corrupt Mexican officials, or were given land as gifts from Mexican authorities. Under Mexican law, it was acceptable for new owners of mission lands to keep Indians on the missions as slaves.

◀ *The Battle of Buena Vista was fought during the Mexican American War.*

Many people came to California searching for gold.

Most of the Ohlone Indians living at Mission San Francisco de Asís left the mission. They moved into San Francisco (which was now a city) or to nearby towns, taking jobs as servants, laborers, cooks, or *vaqueros*. Some tried to return to their former life, but most of their villages had been taken over by missions or settlers. A few formed new settlements away from Mexican towns.

Mexico's rule over Alta California was short. In the 1840s, American settlers flocked to California in search of gold. The new settlers petitioned the United States government to make California a state. American soldiers began to fight with Mexico for control of Alta California in 1846. In 1848, the United States was victorious, and Alta California became a state. It was renamed California in 1850. In the late 1850s, portions of the mission lands in San Francisco were returned to the Roman Catholic Church by an order of the United States president, James Buchanan.

▲
President James Buchanan.

Moving Toward the Present

As the city of San Francisco grew around Mission San Francisco de Asís, some of the mission's buildings were converted into businesses, including a boarding house, a print shop, and several saloons. Parts of the mission grounds were transformed into an arena for bullfights and a racetrack. By 1876, the little chapel was no longer large enough to serve the ever-growing population of San Francisco. A large church was built next to the original chapel and was officially opened on the 100-year anniversary of the founding of Mission San Francisco de Asís. However, in 1906, an earthquake turned the new church to rubble, while the little chapel remained mostly unharmed.

The Chapel

The original chapel, completed in 1791, is the oldest building in San Francisco today. It is 114 feet long and 22 feet wide. The adobe brick walls are four feet thick. Inside, the chapel is decorated with Ohlone and Catholic designs, including geometric and floral patterns and Christian symbols of the cross and the saints. Beams supporting the roof are painted with red, gray, yellow, and white stripes and V-shapes called chevrons. Many of the designs on the walls and support beams were first painted on canvas and then plastered to the walls. The reredos (a large backboard and table used in religious services) covers most of the far wall. Some historians believe that the reredos was carved out of redwood trees native to the San Francisco Bay area. Others believe it was carved in Mexico and transported to Mission San Francisco de Asís in 1796.

The original mission church (on the left) is the oldest building in San Francisco today. ▶

A cemetery is located just south of the chapel and is enclosed by a stone wall. Among palm trees, cacti, and flowers within the walls of the cemetery are grave markers for some of California's first settlers. A statue of Fray Serra stands in the center, along with a memorial statue of an Indian woman. This woman marks the graves of more than 5,000 Indians who were buried on the mission grounds.

Mission Dolores Basilica

After the earthquake in 1906, which leveled the then-new church, the Catholics began building another, even larger, house of worship. This church, currently called Mission Dolores

◀ *This statue reminds visitors of the Indians who gave their lives to the mission.*

▲

Earthquakes caused much damage at the mission.

Basilica, was completed in 1918. It features many architectural designs that are commonly seen in the cathedrals of Europe. In 1952, Pope Pius XII, the head of the Roman Catholic Church, officially designated the church as a basilica. It still serves the surrounding community as a parish church.

Two ornate spires tower above the entrance way. Inside, stained-glass windows line either side of the sanctuary depicting angels, Saint Francis of Assisi, Fray Serra, Fray Palóu, and the 21 Alta California missions.

This diorama is on display at the mission museum.

The Mission Today

Today, Mission San Francisco de Asís is both a tourist attraction and a functioning part of the San Francisco community. In addition to the two churches, the mission contains a museum and gift shop. The museum houses displays of tools, baskets, pottery, and other items that were used by the Spanish missionaries and Ohlone Indians. The museum also contains a diorama depicting the mission complex at its peak during the 1790s. The diorama was made for the World's Fair, held in San Francisco in 1939.

The two churches of Mission San Francisco de Asís stand side by side on Dolores Street in the Mission District of San Francisco. Along the corridor walls leading from one church to the other are sketches and photographs made during different periods of the mission's history. Visitors from around the world come to the mission to catch a glimpse of how the early Californians lived. Influences of the mission period can be seen from San Francisco to San Diego. The San Francisco Bay, spanned by the Golden Gate Bridge, continues to be an important port for trade. Many of the crops first harvested by the Spanish missionaries and American Indians are still being produced today, making California one of the leading agricultural centers in the United States.

The California missions have been the source of both sorrow and celebration throughout their history. They may have been a great conquest for the Spanish, but many see them as a great loss for the California Indian population. Currently, Mission San Francisco de Asís stands in memoriam to all the lives that were lost to make it the monument that it is today.

Make Your Own Mission
San Francisco de Asís

To make your own model of Mission San Francisco de Asís, you will need:

Styrofoam
cardboard
red felt
glue
dry lasagna noodles
glue gun (optional)

Popsicle sticks
toothpicks
red yarn
pins
black and white paint
skill sticks

Directions:

Step 1: Cut out a piece of Styrofoam 10" x 21" for the base.

Adult supervision is suggested.

Step 2: To make the first floor of the church, cut four pieces of Styrofoam 12" by 6.5". Stick the walls together with pins.

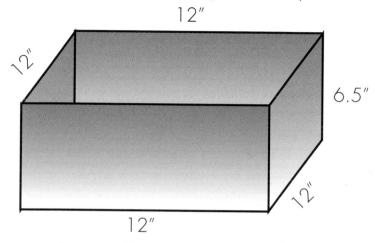

Step 3: Cut two Styrofoam walls measuring 5" x 6.5". Pin them on the left side of the structure.

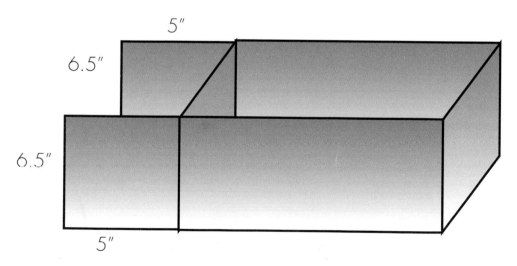

Step 4: To make the second story of the church, cut two 11" by 7" pieces of cardboard. Cut the top corners off, so that the top forms a triangle. The walls should be 4" high.

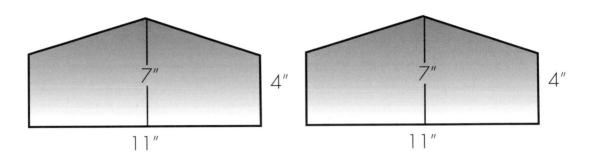

Step 5: Cut out two cardboard side walls measuring 11" by 4". Paint all the pieces of the church's second story white.

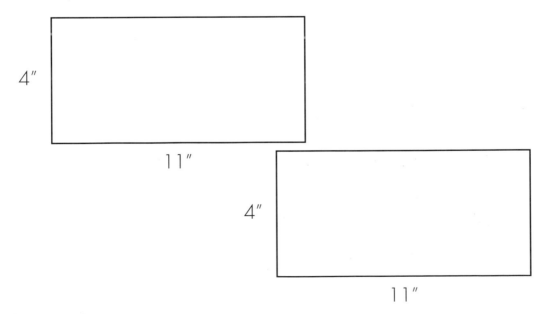

Step 6: Glue the front, back, and side walls together. Attach the second floor to the Styrofoam first floor of the church.

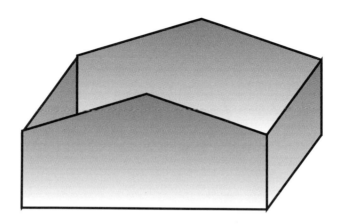

Step 7: For the roof, cut a 20" by 12" piece of cardboard. Bend it in half and glue it in place. Cover the roof with red felt.

20"

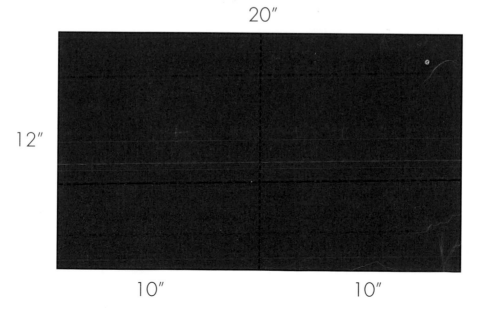

12"

10"   10"

Step 8: For the roof to cover the two small side walls, cut a 12″ by 6″ cardboard piece. Glue lasagna noodles on top. Paint the noodles red.

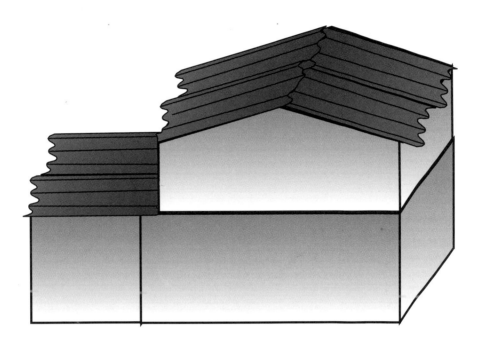

Step 9: Make the balcony by gluing Popsicle sticks and toothpicks to the front of the top floor.

Step 10: To make the lower columns, glue Popsicle sticks to the first floor of the church.

Step 11: To make the top columns, glue sugar cubes to the second story above the balcony.

Step 12: To make windows, cut a Popsicle stick into three pieces, paint these black, and glue onto the top story of the church.

Step 13: Make a cross out of toothpicks and glue it to the roof.

Step 14: To make the doors, cut out a piece of cardboard, paint it, and glue it to the front of the bottom of the church.

Step 15: To decorate the mission grounds, glue on miniature fake trees and bushes.

*Use the above mission as a reference for building your mission.

Important Dates in Mission History

1492	Christopher Columbus reaches the West Indies
1542	Cabrillo's expedition to California
1602	Sebastian Vizcaíno sails to California
1713	Fray Junípero Serra is born
1769	Founding of San Diego de Alcalá
1770	Founding of San Carlos Borromeo del Río Carmelo
1771	Founding of San Antonio de Padua and San Gabriel Arcángel
1772	Founding of San Luis Obispo de Tolosa
1775–76	Founding of San Juan Capistrano
1776	**Founding of San Francisco de Asís**
1776	Declaration of Independence is signed
1777	Founding of Santa Clara de Asís
1782	Founding of San Buenaventura
1784	Fray Serra dies
1786	Founding of Santa Bárbara Virgen y Mártir
1787	Founding of La Purísima Concepción de Maria Santísima
1791	Founding of Santa Cruz and Nuestra Señora de la Soledad
1797	Founding of San José, San Juan Bautista, San Miguel Arcángel, and San Fernando Rey de España
1798	Founding of San Luis Rey de Francia
1804	Founding of Santa Inés Virgen y Mártir
1817	Founding of San Rafael Arcángel
1823	Founding of San Francisco de Solano
1849	Gold found in northern California
1850	California becomes the 31st state

Glossary

adobe (uh-DOH-bee) Sun-dried bricks made of straw, mud, and sometimes manure.

Alta California (AL-tuh kah-lih-FOR-nyuh) The area where the Spanish settled missions, today known as the state of California.

Baja California (BAH-ha kah-lih-FOR-nyuh) The Mexican peninsula directly south of the state of California.

Christian (KRIS-chin) Someone who follows the teachings of Jesus Christ and the Bible.

convert (kun-VURT) To change religious beliefs.

Franciscan (fran-SIS-kin) A communal Roman Catholic order of friars, or "brothers." They follow the teachings and examples of St. Francis of Assisi, who did much work as a missionary.

friar (FRY-ur) A brother in a communal religious order. Friars can also be priests.

granary (GRAY-nuh-ree) A place to store grain.

missionary (MIH-shuh-nayr-ee) A person who teaches his or her religion to people with different beliefs.

neophyte (NEE-oh-fyt) Name for American Indians who were baptized into the Christian faith.

New Spain (NOO SPAYN) The area where the Spanish colonists had their capital in North America, and that would later become Mexico.

sanctuary (SANK-choo-weh-ree) A sacred part of the church containing the altar.

secularization (sek-yoo-luh-rih-ZAY-shun) The process by which the missions went from being religious settlements to non-religious settlements.

Pronunciation Guide

asistencias (a-sis-TEN-see-uhs)

atole (ah-TOH-lay)

campanario (kahm-pahn-AR-ee-oh)

carreta (kah-REH-tah)

fiestas (fee-EHS-tahs)

fray (FRAY)

labor (lah-BOOR)

monjerío (mohn-HAYR-ee-oh)

palizada (pa-lee-ZAH-da)

pozole (po-ZOH-lay)

siesta (see-EHS-tah)

vaqueros (bah-KEHR-ohs)

Resources

To learn more about the California missions and Mission San Francisco de Asís, check out these books and Web sites.

Books:

Boule, Mary. *The Missions: California's Heritage: Mission San Francisco de Asís*. Vashon, WA: Merryant Publishing, 1988.

Giffords, Gloria. *Spanish Colonial Missions*. Southwest Parks and Monument Association, 1988.

Palóu, Francisco. *The Founding of the First California Missions*. San Francisco: Nueva California Press, 1934.

Web Sites:

Newhall Elementary Cyber Serra Virtual Mission Tour
http://www.newhall.k12.ca.us/newhall/cyberserra/cyberserra.htm

Index